PEOPLE WE KNOW

(YOU TO YOURSELF)

SAKSHI PANDIYA

Dedicated to my mom and
my younger self

Contents

Acknowledgements

First, I would like to thank God who gave me an opportunity to write this book because without his blessing it was not possible.
I must thank my grandmother, who is the main reason why I got this idea of writing this book. My grandmother asked me what I wanted to be in future, and I had no answer, so I lied to her that I wanted to be a writer and write books, and that's how one lie became the first step towards writing this book.

I offer my heartfelt gratitude to my mother who inspired me every time whenever I thought of giving up. She is the most strongest woman I have ever seen in my life and she teaches me how to be brave.

I once again thank my mother for sharing her life stories with me which inspired me to write it in my book and share it to the world.

I express my deep sense of gratitude to my guide, Dr. Zeba Siddiqui, who is also my Literature Professor. She spared her precious time in spite of her busy schedule whenever I desired to consult her. Provided invaluable suggestions, therefore, special thanks to my guide.

I thank my friends who some way or other helped me in writing this book and who always stood with me when I needed their support, so thanks to both of them.

Last but not the least, I am grateful to those people who came into my life as a lesson, became the reason of my pain, who made me feel small. I bear you no grudges and I thank you for giving me inspiration for this book.

Sakshi Pandiya

Introduction

This is the very first book I have ever written, and I am very happy to share it with you. It may not be my best work, but I gave my blood, sweat, and tears to write this book. This book is written from my personal experience and from my own perspective, as well as the way this world has been for me. There may be some opinions of mine which you will completely disagree with, and that's totally fine because, as I already said, It's my own perspective.

This book is highly inspired by my college days when I used to have a bunch of friends and when I was just a naïve girl who believed in love and friendship and even thought that fairy tales were real. I used to think all day when my prince charming would arrive on a white horse and take me to his world, and then I'd live happily with him, but little did I know that's where my delusional world was going to end, and I'd face my reality.

YOU AND YOURSELF

YOU AND YOURSELF

You will find a lot of books in the market which talk about self-love and self-belief and many more bullshits. Everyone talks about loving yourself, but no one talks about how to love yourself.

Trust me, as a teenager, I can really relate to the term 'how to love yourself?' because I have been through some shits lately where I totally forgot about myself and was only focused on my problems, but then I realised that my main problem is me, myself.

I am not trying to portray myself as a problem, but I am trying to convey that my focus on my problem was a problem. Instead of focusing on the problem, I should have focused on the solution, or I should just not have given a damn about it, but did I do that? Of course not; your author was very naïve and still is.

There were times when I couldn't think straight and would end up doing something very stupid and unimaginable and it often led to disappointment of many people and I would feel so guilty about making them disappoint. But being guilty is not the option and you don't even have to make up to those people who are disappoint because you are not made for that.

Whenever you do something and someone get disappoint by it just know that they are mad because you didn't work according to them. This world is all about people judging people for something they did for themselves or something which they never expected from them. We can't stop the judgements but we can ignore the judgements.

In this world, the only person you can rely on is yourself, but do you do that? Of course not; you are too busy judging yourself while standing in front of the mirror or probably hating yourself for disappointing people.

The one thing you need to get in your mind is whatever you have is yours nobody else have that and that's the biggest treasure for you. For example, you have a very unique eye shape but some people don't have that and they can't take that away from you cause its yours. I know the example was very bad but that's the only thing I could think off.

As for me I really don't like my smile because it's not a picture-perfect smile but nobody has a smile like me, nobody can smile like me and that's what make me so unique, my smile is something I treasure the most even though I don't like it. I know I sounded a bit self-obsessed but that's how I am. It took me so much efforts to be this obsessed with myself.

Once you start loving yourself, people will tell you lots of things like 'It's not good to be this obsessed with yourself,' 'what does she think of herself,' 'She is too hard to handle.' blah blah shit........ but as I already said ignore it.......

CHAPTER ONE

GET TO KNOW YOURSELF

Getting to know yourself doesn't mean knowing your clothes size or shoe size or your favourite colour or what kind of ice cream flavour you prefer. Getting to know yourself means what kind of living you want and what makes you happy. What makes you sad? And so on.

For me getting to know myself is taking care of myself and spoiling myself to that depth that I start enjoying my own company. sometimes you may feel lonely but trust me its better staying that way instead of gossiping about some random person who doesn't have any importance in your life.

Gossiping will never make you learn about yourself because you are showing too much interest in others' lives rather than yours. The only gossip you should do is about yourself. If you don't have any company, go in front of the mirror and talk to yourself. You'll feel better after talking to yourself, and you won't be afraid of someone misusing your gossip about you. (I know that was lame)

You have to figure out what kind of environment you like and what kind of people and company you enjoy; we all make the mistake of making friends without any background check, now you will tell me that this is such a rude comment, how am I supposed to make friends with a background check, I don't have that much time etc ...

When I said background check means their behaviour check. Whether they are cool minded or filled with anger issues. I am not telling you go and check how much property they have or how many girlfriends and boyfriends they have. If you want to love yourself you got to make good friends who have positive mindset and are always active.

We all have or had a friend who was always negative minded and used to think all the bad possibilities that could happen to him. That's where you have to realise that it's time to let go that friend or if you want to do social service then go and try to change him but if you want my advice then I would recommend not to do any social servicing because that's not your job.

You have to live your life like you don't owe anything to anyone. It's hundred per cent true that you don't owe anything to anyone except the money you borrowed from your best friend [it's a reminder to return the money to your friend]. My good advice for you is that don't let money come between your friendship.

I remembered a quote which says 'Live like a King or live like you don't care who is the King,' and this quote doesn't mean that go and command everyone and punish them. you live a good life like a king who is kind and helping to his subject.

CHAPTER TWO

TYPES OF PEOPLE IN YOUR LIFE

In this world there are lots of people you know, be it your relative, friend, family or neighbour and the list goes on, but do you notice one thing that not every one of them have importance in your life. Only few people from the above are very close to you and that's nothing weird about it.

In your life you will meet a lot of people some will stay and some will not, and that's completely normal, you don't have to worry about those people who didn't stay in your life instead focus on those people who are with you at the exact moment.

In my college time, when no one was talking to me, I felt very bad, and I even cried to my mom about it, but my mom told me that this is just the start. You will lose many people now.

One thing I realised is that the more honest you are, the more they dislike you. Some people really don't like to admit their mistakes; they just want to look like a perfect angel while committing sins like the devil.

Always remember that everyone has a different side which they don't want the world to know, they keep hiding this personality of them because they too know that this wouldn't turn out good if they show this personality to people. I always wonder why people do this? I mean why they hide their real personality?

The answer is simple that they don't want to feel left out, they can do anything just to fit in the standard, so they can appear more likeable in front of them. They can do anything to be loved and faking their personality is one of them.

You have to be very careful with such people because they can go to any extent just to feed themselves, even if it means hurting you. If you don't feed them, they will go somewhere else where they get fed properly and there, they will start spreading lies about you and will try to destroy your reputation.

In today's world everyone cares about their reputation, reputation is the weakness of every human being. reputation is so delicate that it takes years to build a reputation but it won't even take few minutes to destroy it.

Not only me, but I guess all parents tell their children not to share their weaknesses with anyone, no matter how close they are to that person, because it won't take a second for those people to turn into their enemies. What after that?

Isn't it clear that they will use your weakness against you? Now the question is, why does this happen? There might be two reasons.

First: they were never your close friend {from their perspective}

Second, you did something which they didn't like and chose to be against you.

If you like something, just go and get it or start the process of getting that thing. Don't tell the whole planet that you see it, you like it, and you want it; you are not Ariana Grande. Instead of wasting your energy on talking about what you want, why don't you give that energy to getting it? Life would be easier.

Never flaunt your precious things in front of people because trust me people really don't like it when the precious thing is not theirs.

My dad once told me that some people are your friends because they are too scared to be your enemy. They only envy you and the power that you hold. He also told me that there are people who only acts like they pray good for you but the reality is something else.

Some people are devil from mind and angel from face. No matter how much you try to avoid these types of people they will appear in your life at least once, and I wish they appear in your life so you can learn your lesson and move on with great intention of uprising your life.

Now you will think what kind of writer she is? she wants these people to appear in my life. Then yes, I want them to appear in your life because by reading this book you won't be a perfect person but by experiencing such situations you may find a right path and will be able to move forward in your life.

IGNORE THEIR OPINION

If you want to be that bad b!tch who is obsessed with herself and her personality, the first thing you need to do is stop being a stupid idiotic people-pleaser, you have to be a straight forward b!tch.

This straightforward trait of yours will become a problem to others, but it will benefit you as you will no longer make any excuses to feed them. Never agree with such a decision you are uncomfortable with, and always stand strong about your decision.

I just want you to be true to yourself and the people who you love and who loves you. Just make a promise with yourself that you will never break your heart by your own.

If you get negative vibes from some person and your gut feeling tells you to stay away from them, then bitch stay away from them because your guts are more intelligent than you. You are just a dumb idiot person who knows nothing about such people, but don't worry; your guts are there to help you.

No matter what happened never look down on yourself, you are the most unique person not for others but for yourself you are the most beautiful and talented person. There will be times when people will look down on you and will make you feel worthless. but their judgement doesn't define you and your worth. The best thing you can do to yourself is to stay away from such people who are small minded.

One of the most important things to remember is that never share your insecurities to other person, because they will not pity you or will give you opportunities to prove your worth, when the time will come to show your worth, they'll be the one to point out your insecurities and make you feel worthless.

You may not be the boss but at least you are b!tch, being b!tch to the people who deserve it is not a bad thing because sometimes they should get the taste of their own medicine.

Sometimes, it's necessary to stay silent in some situations, not because if you talk, you'll mess up but because your opinions are very precious, so give them to precious people and important situations.

You live your life on your own terms, not on someone else's condition. As BTS already said, 'Live as you want; it's your life anyway,' honey, Even Devi Vishwa Kumar from *Never Have I Ever* said, "My mom doesn't tell me how to live, but Meghan Thee Stallion does."

Sometimes, you will not be able to figure out what's happening in your life, but that doesn't mean it's the end of your life; it's just your hormones. [Sorry for this terrible joke]

In the end, just don't do something which make you lose your smile. your smile is precious don't fade it because of some useless opinion given by some useless people.

YOU AND YOUR FAMILY

YOU AND YOUR FAMILY

In this world, if we ask a person what is important to him or her, he or she would definitely say one of these words: 'family.' Of course, who wouldn't think of their family as important?

Family is where a person can be free and can be his true self. family is where a person doesn't have to think twice to put his opinion and where he can have good company.

In a family we have our parents who loves us unconditionally but with some condition, for example some parents think their child is not working according to them then he is a bad child. You cannot have an opinion of your own even if the situation is about you or related to you.

As for me, it has always been my parents to whom I listen, and when I don't listen to them, I am labelled as the bad child and often treated as the black sheep. If I speak for myself, then BANGG! GAME OVER

Most of the parents, especially Indian parents, keep their children in control in the name of protection. Many think that keeping their child in control is parenting. If parents cannot provide peace to their children, then they should not have given birth to them.

Giving birth doesn't make you parents; it takes guts to be a parent because I personally think that once you become a parent, you can never be a good daughter/son or sibling. Once you become parents, your attention should be on your child because if you don't give them attention, they'll seek it from somewhere else.

Our parents tell us that they always hold us in high regard and never think badly of us, and I completely agree with this. Sometimes, they need to understand that they are thinking well for us, but the way they think can be wrong. If the child doesn't like what you want for him, then parents should not force them.

By forcing them to agree with your decision, you are just growing hate in children mind for you. As I mentioned previously being parents needs guts not anyone can be a parent. I mean everyone can be a parent but not everyone can be a good parent.

If I ever want to become a parent, the first thing I'll do is to go to therapy because if I go to therapy, my children don't have to. [not a joke but a fact.]

CHAPTER FOUR

BLOOD DOESN'T MEAN FAMILY

Now-a-days you can see that siblings are fighting among them for property and maybe fighting with their parents. The world has become very selfish in the matter of materialistic things, things are more loved by people than people itself.

Today, nobody values relationships as they are too absorbed in valuing money and the position they have. Trust me not everybody who is your blood is your family, be careful with such people who values money more than people.

If you don't believe me, then let me tell you the story of my parents; this happened when I was not born. My mother was pregnant with my big brother, and my parents used to live in a joint family.

At that time, my father's income was just 1500 rupees per month, and it was the end of the month, and there was nothing to eat in the house. My mother was starving to death; my dad was outside to get some money so that he could feed his wife.

My mother was in the kitchen crying with the thought that she and her unborn child both are hungry, but outside the kitchen in the hall, my father's relatives were eating biryani, drinking and watching TV even after knowing that my brother's wife was starving. My mother slept while crying as she could not handle the hunger.

This shows that blood doesn't mean family. I knew it you won't believe me because I am just a teenager that's why I gave you example of my parents as they have experienced things more than I have.

There is one more incident that proves my words right, my father and his brother opened a shop in partnership my father invested a huge amount of money in that shop. He brought money from my mom's uncle and sister. As we see in many old Bollywood movies where the partner betrays the main character, same thing happened with my father too.

He got betrayed by his partner, and he was left all in debt, and nobody helped him. Before this incident happened, my dad went to Bangalore to earn money, so we had to move to the village as we could not afford to stay in Mumbai as well as Bangalore.

Not to brag, but because of the shortage of money, I studied in a government school, and I let my siblings study in a good school; even though my mother didn't force me, I knew the circumstances and understood the situation and tried my best to not to be a burden on my parents. I used to tutor my big brother and small sister, so it saved the tuition fees, and my parents could use it to pay the debt.

Now, after six years, we are financially good, but that partner of dad hasn't returned the money to my dad, so if that uncle is reading this book, then please return the money to my dad. I want to plan a trip to Paris. {I'm just joking, but do return the money.}

Sometimes, the person who is your blood may not be the one who supports you in every situation; a complete stranger can be the one who will support you no matter what and will be by your side.
Not all the blood is bad. My dad's oldest sister was there for my father in every situation, good or bad. The fact that she is no longer with us upsets me, but I pray that her soul rests in peace.

My father and she had a very good bond. When we first came to Mumbai, I was just 5 years old. She was the one who gave us shelter and helped us to settle in Mumbai. She helped us even though she had her own problems. My father misses her every day and sometimes he cries while recollecting all the moments with her.

This shows a pure form of love between siblings. sometimes its blood which make a family and sometimes its love.

CHAPTER FIVE

A REAL DAMAGE

A family can be a real damage if it's toxic; like I mentioned previously, family is not everyone's safe place. Trauma is passed from generation to generation unless someone decides to break the generation trauma cycle. In the introduction of this part, I talked about parenting. However, parenting is related to trauma.

Today, only very few people are mentally strong and healthy; most people have suffered from some problems, which is why there is a high chance that they have stored trauma inside them. These trauma leads people to trust issues, anger issues, people pleasing and many more.

When these types of people who have stored trauma inside them become parents, they just pass on their traumas to their children. Sometimes, you may think that the father and daughter duo are the same in terms of personality. Well, it's more like the same in terms of trauma. Mental health is also important as much as physical health.

Parents with traumas can be emotionally or physically abusive towards their children. The child can never detect the abuse coming from the parents as they take that abuse in the form of care and parents protection. This type of relationship between children and parents is known as trauma bonding.

A trauma bond is formed when the child is stuck in the cycle of abuse and love. For example, after the abuse, parents would show lots of love and care for the child. Many children get the hope that their parents will change, but they never change, and the cycle of trauma bond continues.

I will never blame anyone for this, as it's natural for traumas to pass on from generation to generation unless one decides to heal and end the cycle. I know this quote which says, "If you don't heal what hurt you, you will bleed on people who didn't cut you." This one quote can explain the concept of the trauma cycle.

Some parents never tolerate being wrong about anything, they will defend themselves and will make excuses for their behaviour and will gaslight their children. They will always make the child feel that he is the reason why they behaved in such way.

Before, I never knew that my parents also had trauma stored inside them, but after reaching a certain maturity, I see that not only my parents but also my grandparents have trauma inside them. My grandparents never worked on their trauma, so it was passed on to my parents.

These types of parents are emotionally unavailable. Imagine not showing up for your child when he needs you the most. This experience makes the child lonely and emotionally independent. They don't show any emotions as they think nobody will help them. For a child his parents are the support system but sometimes despite having a support system they have to be independent.

I remembered my parent never came to drop me to school and to pick me from school as soon as I entered the first grade. I never complaint about it because I never thought it was a problem since my mom was busy taking care of her mother-in-law and dad was busy in earning and providing.

In fourth grade, I went to a picnic at my school, and one day before the picnic, I requested my mom to come and pick me up from school after I returned from the picnic as my friend's mom was also coming to pick her up. I came back from a picnic; I was standing at the gate of my school, waiting for my mom as she promised me she would come and pick me up. My friend told me to go along with her, but I refused, and I told her with a big smile on my face that mom was coming to pick me up.

She said she will wait for me until my mother comes, I guess she already knew that my mom will not come that's why she waited for me. After waiting for certain period, I lost all hope and went with my friend and her mother. As I entered my buildings society, I saw my mom chatting with some ladies and I felt very bad but I ignored it and never spoke about that incident to my mother.

Maybe the intentions were not real, but the damage was real.

CHAPTER SIX

TOXIC IS TOXIC

We should not tolerate any toxic behaviour, even if it's your own family; nobody in the world has the right to mess with your mental health. People become toxic due to their past trauma and experiences. A toxic person can be anyone who adds negativity to your life. A person who makes your life hard is also a toxic person. Better cut them off from your life.

Such people are manipulative, abusive and selfish. Toxic people may be your family members, neighbours, friends, etc. Some common behaviours of toxic people include constant criticism, gaslighting and a need for power and control. If you point out their behaviour to their attention, they may criticise you for having issues with their behaviour.

They will falsely portray themselves as the victim and you as the abuser. They don't care about your feelings; they will constantly gaslight you and make you question your own worth. The constant tension you experience from a toxic person affects your mind and body. Toxic people disrespect emotional and physical boundaries. {reference link of above paragraphs www.psychologytoday }

Toxic is toxic no matter who the person is, and it will be very hard to survive with them if you keep on tolerating their behaviour. Once you let them disrespect your boundaries, they won't stop there. They will continue with their behaviour until you are left with no energy. Toxic people drain your energy and leave you exhausted.

Detaching yourself from such people is a step you should take to protect yourself and your mental health. Lord Krishna says, "Koi vyakti chahe kitna bhi khaas kyon na ho use ek pal me tyaagne ki shamata tum mai avashya honi chahiye," which translates to "No matter how special a person is, you must have the ability to abandon him in a moment."

Some people emotionally blackmail us to make us stay in their lives, but we must abandon them if they are using us to heal themselves and drain us; these types of people are very dangerous. About all this toxicity, I don't blame anyone.

Before I used to feel bad about it that why they treated me that way but now I don't feel anything as they also did everything that they could do for me and as a child I forgive them but as a human I can never forgive them.

Don't hold grudges; forgive-and-forget.

YOU AND YOUR FRIENDS

YOU AND YOUR FRIENDS

Before we get into the topic, I want to ask you what is a friend for you? Or what kind of person do you think should be your friend? For me a friend is always a person who thinks good about you or helps you. Some friends will just show you that they are helping us but they are not helping us.

Some friends help you because they think they can get it back from you, so basically, they are not helping you but doing a favour for you. A real friend will help you because he wants to help you, not because he wants to show-off that he helped you.

In your life you will meet many people who will claim that they are your friend or best friend and probably this stupid word 'BFF' which means best friend forever but, in a minute, you become the most arrogant person and any other random person becomes their 'BFF.'

Some people be friends with you because of your status, beauty, popularity and many more, only few people really see the nature and your inner self to be friends with you. Nobody becomes your friend because they want to understand you but they want you to understand them.

Suppose a girl is very beautiful and most popular girl in the college or anywhere; at that point, everyone wants to be friends with her even if she is dumb and doesn't have any common sense, but people still want to be with her, because why not? she is pretty and popular.

Now-a-days friendships are made by matching status. In today's date status is more valuable than personality. The standards are set high for a friendship but there is no genuine bonding, everyone is using each other for their own sake and stability.

Not everybody deserves you, so be wise while making friends and if you are already friends with someone make sure that they treat you the way you want to be treated. Don't sacrifice anything for any of your friend unless you are sure that your bond is genuine.

Be aware of snake friends who enjoys your misery and congratulate you on your loss and will help you to destroy your life in a very polite way and will never apologise for all the things they did to you. For them it's fun and satisfaction but for you it's your life don't let them play with your life, it's your duty to look after yourself and protect yourself from such people.

Staying alone is way better than staying with someone who only knows how to add misery to your life and will always come up with new ideas on how to make sure that you are living the most miserable life.

Not everyone is like that, some people are there who really wants a genuine friendship and a friend through the highs and lows. A friend, who is there when they need them most and be there for their friend when they need them. A friend with no jealousy just pure love and support is all a person desire for.

In the process of making a genuine friend you will meet a lot of people who will pretend to be your friend but make sure you don't forget to love yourself because if not anyone than you can become your own friend.

CHAPTER SEVEN

WHAT IS A REAL FRIEND?

A real friend is very hard to find but once you find it just know that you earned something more worthy than money and status. A real friend will try to make you feel you are the only one in this world and will try to make your life easy. They will make sure you are having the best time of your life with them.

'A friend in need is a friend indeed' the very famous proverb defines that when you are falling apart the one who rescue you is your true friend because we all know in darkness even our shadow leaves us but a true friend will never leave us no matter what the situation is.

I would like to give you an example about friendship which you may find lame but believe me the hurt was real. I was in seventh grade, I shifted to village because of financial condition and I made a new friend with whom I eventually got very close and we became best friend.

I was literally ready to do anything for her and I thought she also feels the same. We used to hangout every day and it was very fun and heartwarming to be with her. Her mom started treating me as her own daughter and my mom was very happy that I made a friend and same goes for me.

We were in the same school but not in the same class she was one class ahead from me. One day she forgets to bring her journal and I went to buy journal for her without her knowledge. I left my lecture and went to buy the journal for her.

I bought the journal and gave it to her; she didn't utter a single word, not even a thank you. I thought she would feel good that I made an effort for her, but I let it slide and went back to my class. After school, her classmates told me that she was taking me for granted and not to be with her. She was not good for me, but I ignored it as I thought they were manipulating me.

The next day, I wanted to ask her if she is comfortable with this friendship, so I went to her class and I accidentally eavesdrop her saying that I show-off that I am a good friend but I am not and she also said that she is just pitying me because I don't have friends and she cursed at me. That was the moment I realised that her class mates were right.

I felt very hurt, after that day I stopped talking to her, I used to feel sad that I wanted to talk to her so badly but I couldn't because she deserves my ignorance. After few days I thought of forgiving her and continue our friendship but she had a different plan.

I saw her with her new best friend, I don't know why but I felt very stupid and I straight away went to home and cried to my mom about all this thing. She consoled me and told me that you will meet many friends that will be better than her. You cannot cry over a person who don't give you any importance.

One day she came to me and said sorry to me and as a stupid girl I am, I accepted her apology and gave her a second chance and so she introduced me with her new friend and we became a trio only in front of people deep inside in this friendship I was the outcast.

I would always feel neglected and I would feel uncomfortable whenever I was with them because I was never involved in any of their plans. One day, we all were joking, and I accidentally said something {I don't remember what I said as this happened years ago}. She became furious, and I apologised immediately, and she showed her true colour.

She didn't accept the apology and started shouting at me and crying. {I guess I said something very rude anyway she deserves it}

I was shocked by the way she was playing the victim role, and that's where she said all the things on my face she told her classmates about me.

Some days went by, and everything became okay except our friendship but I didn't pay any attention to it, she would intentionally come in front of me with her so-called best friend and would taunt me and would try teach me moral values of friendship and I would ignore it but sometimes I could not endure it and would cry. Seeing me cry they would make fun of me and that was really heart breaking.

This is how a heartwarming friendship turned into a heartbreaking one. I maintained my distance from her and tried my best not to be involved with her again even though she apologised, but I knew that she was never going to change. I cannot continue this hot and cold friendship pattern as I know I will be the one who will always end up miserable.

I am ready to live alone, but I am not ready to live with someone who can destroy me. I don't want to live with such people just because I don't want to feel left out. Being left out is the best thing that can happen to you; it's a blessing in disguise.

TOXIC FRIEND CIRCLE

Have you ever caught yourself in a group of friends where no one is no one's friend? Or a group that exists only on the basis of show-off and reputation? Well I did catch myself and it left me with a low self-esteem and reminded me that I am better off alone.

This part of my life was the most memorable part as it taught me more about the real world and broke my delusional world. I once again put my whole faith in a bunch of friends just to get the faith shattered. If I had known this, I would have saved myself from them, but I couldn't.

If I had saved myself from them, I would have never learned the lesson that God was trying to teach me. God will keep sending such people into your life until you learn your lessons and stop repeating the same mistakes.

When you feel like you do not fit in the standard of the group and you feel bad about it, just look at that group's each and every single member and ask yourself a question: do you think they have any future?' or 'do you think they are ambitious?' Then look at yourself and ask the same questions.

If you think, you don't have any future and they also don't have any future then there's no single way that you didn't fit in that group and if you think you are ambitious and they are not then its normal to not fit in the that group.

There's a ninety- nine per cent chance to appear unlikeable to them if you are being your true self, but there is a one per cent chance to be likeable by faking your personality. I already talked about how faking your personality to fit in any group is the worst thing you can do to yourself.

You are literally making friends on the base of something which is not true and it might create a problem for you in future. I don't think your self would be proud of you knowing that you are not acknowledging your true self but trying to be someone you are not.

If you look at a toxic friend circle, they are most likely to appear a picture-perfect friend circle but behind the scene there are many things that you are not aware of. They all have one thing in common that is they don't have a genuine bond that's why its toxic.

They all talk about each other behind their back and when they are altogether, they act like they are inseparable, they try to show-off that we are the most lovable and supporting friend circle.

If you look carefully at all these groups, there is a leader who does not have a status; unconsciously, everyone thinks of that particular person as the leader because he makes all the plans and leads the group.

The leader of the group is always well-settled and the others are not, I don't know about other groups but from my personal experience the leader are always settled in their life. The group in which I once was a part also had a leader who was rich and settled while the others came from middle-class families.

The second friend group which I almost joined but thanks to God that I didn't because my intuition told me that only the people are change but the lesson will be same, so I backed off. I trusted my intuition and my intuition never lies they all are were a bad influence to my life.

In that group, the leader was also well-settled, financially stable, and had no worries about the future, and the others were ordinary people from middle-class families. In almost every group, there is a particular person who unconsciously ruins others' lives. I thank God every day for helping me learn my lesson and see the truth.

CHAPTER NINE

THE BLAME

I had these so-called friends who blamed me for everything; they would always complain that it was not their fault that they had to take those steps, which hurt me just because I wasn't acting right. Like seriously, go fool somebody else.

Even after putting up with their shitty behaviour, I was the one who wasn't acting right. I remember the time when I had lots of restrictions, but I dreamed of becoming a dancer, as many people said I had this talent. So, I asked my friend I had a plan: I would join a dance class, and I would open my YouTube channel.

Do you know what he said? He said, "It's impossible. Don't even try; just marry a guy and settle." I felt like giving a tight slap to his already ugly face, but I controlled myself and let it slide. Then I intentionally asked him that do you think I can be a singer? And his reply was the same as his ugly face: "Yes, you can, you can be a bar singer."

I don't think so we need such types of friends in our lives who only know how to demotivate us. After that day, I maintained my distance, but I couldn't, as he was my classmate, too. I remember paying for him so many times. {anyway, I love donating}

There are so many times I felt uncomfortable with that particular group the way they treated me was something I didn't liked at all.

Once, we were just eating pizza, and I didn't have any money to pay, so one girl in the group was glaring at me like she was about to kill me if I didn't pay the money.

The very next day I gave money to that girl because I don't want any favours especially from such people. Well, I am surrounded by people who seriously have such a fake personality. I have this friend of mine. She is so fake like she would spam my WhatsApp with her lovely texts but when she will see me in real, she won't even look at me and will hang out with other friends.

I seriously feel so stupid that sometimes I think that maybe I am the problem. When I reflect on my past none of the friendship I had worked out and I would blame myself for being the reason no one could stay with me for a long period, but now I look at myself and I feel blessed that I have a friend who is real to me.

Do you know the pain of not being the priority of a person who is our priority? Well, I do know.

I remember an incident that happened in my school.

I was in fourth grade and English lecture was going on and we were studying letter writing so the question was "write a letter to your best friend" and I wrote my best friends name but she wrote her other best friends' name.

I felt hurt and I was angry too so I stop talking to her. After some days in English lecture the teacher was explaining the poem 'Little Words' which is a poem about two friends having a quarrel and apologising, and continuing their friendship.

After the lecture was over, she immediately came to me and apologised to me. She said she is feeling bad about not writing my name on the letter. She even wrote an apology letter to me that was really heartwarming to read and I forgive her. She was really good friend of mine but I shifted that's why I lost my contact with her.

Sometimes apologising for your mistakes can save your friendship but if you didn't do any mistakes and they want you to feel sorry then don't do it because there is a different between accepting your mistake and diminishing your self-respect.

YOU AND YOUR LOVERS

YOU AND YOUR LOVERS

What is the first thing you think of when you hear the word lover? Probably a six-foot-tall, handsome man who will make you his queen and will love you till his death. If that's what you think, then sister, please wake up from that dream.

A lover is not all about loving you its more than that because if he loves you but he cannot understand you than what is the point of loving. if your lover cannot understand you, try communicating with them; maybe they will understand. However, if they still cannot understand after you've communicated, it may be best to stop there. There is no need to invest more energy in trying to make them understand.

Everyone has different style of showing their love some people like to spoil their partner with all their riches while some like to whisper soothing words to their partner. The main key to love is trust and understanding. We all see many couples where the one person is overprotective over the other, many people call it as care but I will say its lack of trust and their own insecurities.

People with insecurities are always afraid of their partner leaving them that's why they make these toxic boundaries around their partner to keep them in the line. They want their partner to enjoy their life but only with them. They want their partner to give access only to them not to any of their friends. What's crazier is that people take this behaviour as love but I will always say its toxic.

Some people want complete freedom. They cannot live in such a toxic environment, so they separate from their partner, but that insecure partner can do anything to make them stay. They will threaten them that they will kill themselves if the partners leave them.

I don't think this is love, this is pure toxicity and that person needs to find a good therapist. If you don't feel comfortable with your partner then please tell your partner that you don't feel comfortable about this particular act of them. Communication is the key of any relationship; the right one will always listen to you and will understand you.

I would like to suggest that one should always reflect at their own red flags and it's okay if you find yourself toxic, nobody is perfect and nobody will but you can try to be better than the person you were before.

Once you discover any of your red flags, try to work on them, heal your traumas and find a good therapist if you can. Mental health is the best thing yet the worst thing because if you understand how to be mentally healthy, then it's good, but if it's not, and if it's filled with traumas, then it's the worst thing.

Some people don't understand how our mental health can affect all the things in our lives. Be it our physical health or our personality, everything is dependent on our mental health. Mental health can literally control the way we act and react to any situation in our lives.

Mental health is very important; if your mental health is ruined, then you will even accept poor treatment from other people, you will lack self-respect, and you will also lack the understanding of good and bad and will do something which can make your life full of struggles.

You should not take your mental health for granted; taking care of your mental health should be your first priority. Moreover, don't give anyone enough power to mess with your mental health.

You are the only person who has the power to decide anything for you and choose wisely who you should make your lover. Not everybody deserves your love.

CHAPTER TEN

ATTRACTION OR LOVE?

Have you ever heard the word 'crush?' Or sentence like 'I have a crush on that guy?' Well you can't say no because everyone in their teenage had a crush on someone. Having a crush on someone is a normal phase of our teenage life and its completely fine to have crush on someone.

Well, I had lots of crushes when I hit my puberty and I would literally change my crush like changing photos in a frame. The crush phase is the first phase of your real life because that's when you understand a little bit about how the world works.

I had a crush on a guy who was so handsome and had a well-built body, a perfect smile, and a deep voice. Hc had cvcrything a girl looks for in a boy, but he was not doing financially well, and of course , I , didn't mind that at all. I thought that he was my true love, and I was head over heels for him.

He knew that I like him and would give me mix signals but some of my friends got to know about his personality which was clearly the opposite of his looks. He looked like a daydream but his personality was a nightmare. I remember writing songs for him in my book and I would do love test, make fake scenarios about him, I even imagined my wedding with him.

Now, after so many years, I look back in time and laugh at all the stupid things I would do when I was in my crush phase. I feel embarrass whenever I think about those things but I accept it as a part of my life which made me into a person I am today .

This is not the only part of my life where reality hit me; there are dozens of such incidents which made me face my reality. There was one guy who literally threatened me that he would kill himself if I didn't agree to date him and would spread lies about me being his girlfriend.

Some guys will only date you because they feel attracted to you physically and you would think that he loves me for who I am. In today's world genuine love is rare to find, everyone is attracted to someone by their physical things be it appearance, status or wealth.

My friend recently went through a relationship where the boy was very proud of her participating in the fashion show and would flaunt her in front of his friend and that's not something bad but what is bad is that he claims himself a sigma male.

He also thought her as an ornament that he can flaunt and only date her because she has a good reputation and she is really beautiful and popular. He would also invade her personal space by showing up at her workplace.

In some relationships the attraction is so dangerous that they manipulate their partner to stay with them. They would always do something which will disappoint their partner and then instead of apologising they will manipulate them into thinking that it is not the way they are thinking.

We can also include the hot and cold behaviour that one person gives to their partner, they would literally make them feel so special in the start and then would treat them like they don't even exist.

Therefore, there is a huge difference between love and attraction.

Love is freedom while attraction is attachment. Love is permanent while attraction is temporary. I don't know more about love as I have never been in love but I do believe that love exist and it will find your way one day and that day your happiness will multiply.

CHAPTER ELEVEN

YOU OR YOUR ATTENTION?

Let me tell you a story that is considered very normal in society, but it is not. Have you heard a story where there is a main character and her boyfriend and the main character's close friend? The boyfriend cheats on the main character with her close friend.

Well, this thing happens to so many people. Some forgive, some don't, some date someone better than them to make them jealous, some move on and live a good life, some can't move on and keep themselves in the darkness for years as they are too hurt to forgive them and too attached to move on.

Such people need to understand that leaving them is better than punishing them because it does not matter to them at all. If you matter to them, they would never do something that could hurt you. I am not experienced in these matters, but I did face something similar to this incident. It was not my friend, but it was my cousin.

When we were young, she would always borrow my clothes and other accessories; many times, she stole my lipsticks. [I know it's funny] Till accessories and clothes, I din't mind, but she crossed the boundaries.

I didn't want to mention this incident, but I couldn't stop myself from sharing it because she thought I didn't know anything about it. Well, if she gets married to that guy in future, I will definitely let you know. Guys, stay tuned.

I would also recreate that scene from 'Marry My Husband' a Korean drama where the main character tells the girl, "Congratulations for picking up my trash." If she got married, I would definitely congratulate her. After all, she is my lovely cousin [note the sarcasm].

I know that she is not the only one in fault that guy is also at fault but I will blame her more because she is my cousin and he is just a mere guy. I told you that I used to believe in fairytales and many things happened which gave me a reality check about how the world works.

My own best friend became a prey of such guy who literally broke up with her and dated other girl the very next day and I don't know how but the other girl left that guy after two days only. [karma is real] but he didn't stop there he dated another girl the very next day.

I was astonished by the way he was playing this stupid game so smoothly. I don't know what was his problem but I guess he was scared of being lonely or the reason was something else. That's why I told you be wise while choosing your partner.

Some people can't see you happy with others so they try their best to create a false narrative of you and present them in front of other people. By doing this they try to make people hate you but you don't need to pay attention to such people because when the fox can't get the grapes, he thinks they are sour.

Today, the world is so different that boys want princess treatment compared to girls. Like they want the girl to give them flowers and buy them whatever they want. A boy wants princess treatment while a man wants to give princess treatment; there is a huge difference between a man and a boy.

Well, I don't think spending money on your man is a bad thing, but make sure that he deserves it.

CHAPTER TWELVE

AGAIN, THE BLAME!

I don't know who to blame for the way I am right now! Should I blame my parents for giving me childhood trauma, that's why I was left with this people-pleaser personality or should I blame my ex-friends that because of them, I was left with no self-esteem, or should I blame my ex-lovers for making me realise that Disney prince doesn't exist or should I blame myself for trusting them and following them blindly.

In the end, I still don't know who to blame or who is responsible; maybe I should not ignore my own red flags and believe that at some point in my life, I did hurt people because they did the same to me. I was never a forgive-and-forget kind of girl, but I realise that this is only a waste of time and energy. Instead, I should focus on something which can benefit me and this world in a good way.

Instead of planning revenge lets plan a trip to Paris with yourself or your friends. Whenever you feel like taking revenge just think that "are those people going to matter to you in five years?" if not then that's the sign that you should forgive everything, they did to you.

If you don't want to forget that than its okay but don't let that particular incident haunt you for the rest of your life. You are here to enjoy your life not to stress about your life. don't stress about your life because of other people who don't matter to you.

The truth is that you cannot escape the things which are going to happen to you but you can definitely escape the outcomes of what has already happened. don't pay attention to those things or people which doesn't matter to you because there are many other things and people to focus on.

Sometimes we blame the situations for what we are now or we will blame the whole universe for making such situations. We need to know that blaming others will never solve your problem or blaming the situation or blaming anything for your condition will never make your condition better.

It will just become worse as you are giving your energy in the blaming not in figuring out the main cause of the misery. The misery is always not because of others, sometimes it starts by you and you could not handle the results and then you start blaming the whole universe.

The universe didn't do anything it's just you who make dumb decisions on your emotions not from your brain. Sometimes people will blame you for the wrong things they did to you but that doesn't make you a bad person it's just that they are very coward to accept their mistakes and will blame it on you and will play a victim role.

The worst you can do to yourself is playing a victim role because nobody cares about what you have been through. nobody is interested in knowing your struggle story everybody will look at the success only. If you keep quite then you are a good person but if you speak up for yourself then you are trouble.

Just because they will call you trouble that doesn't mean you will not speak up for yourself. You have to speak up for yourself no matter what, promise yourself that even if nobody is on your side you will still speak up for yourself.

YOU AND THE WORLD

YOU AND THE WORLD

Have you ever asked yourself that why everything is happening to me only? Or why this world is so unfair for me? I bet you did ask yourself these types of questions every time when you are stuck in any situation. Well, questioning yourself is a human nature and is not an alien concept.

Everyone doubts themselves in many situations, but you need to be confident enough to face the world. The world was unfair to everyone, and it will be unfair to you, too, but that should not stop you from living your purposeful life.

The world can affect you in many ways either bad or good, you can also affect the world but make sure to affect the world in a good way. The world is not a safe place for everyone so they always stay in their delusional life, enjoying their own life with their own terms.

If you think, the world is all yours and every opportunity is yours, you just need the courage to face the world, which will always criticize you for everything. As Priyanka Chopra said, "No matter what you do, someone will always be unhappy."

The world has two sides, the good side and the bad side; on the good side, people are always in the front appreciating your efforts, and the bad side will always criticise your efforts. One thing you need to know is that you cannot please everyone in this world, so find your community where you fit in, where you are respected, where you are heard, and where you are appreciated.

No matter how much you change or put efforts to change this world, you will never be appreciated by everyone, so you have to accept this fact that you are going to get criticised by some portion of people. Changing the world has always been a hard task even for God.

Even gods were criticised for trying to change the world then we are just human. If you can't change the world in a good manner then you don't have the right to create nuisance in this world.

Today's world is divided into so many parts that humans are fighting among themselves in the name of religion, caste, gender and many more. There are many problems going on in this world, but the one who is most affected is women.

No matter what happens in the world, women always suffer. Due to a gender-biased society, women always suffer; they constantly face inequality and disrespect from their own families. The patriarchal mindset has killed the dreams of women.

Today women have their own rights but no freedom. They have the right to do a job but they don't have the freedom to do a job. They have the right to education but are not allowed to study.

The world is so globalised that today, most people have a good mindset, and they treat everyone with equal respect. Even though the world has developed, some things have never changed, like some old traditions which are not suitable for humankind.

We live in this world and it's our responsibility to create a better world for us and the upcoming generation. Let's promise ourself that if we cannot preserve the world than we should not destroy it.

CHAPTER THIRTEEN

WHY THEM?

First of all, you all know that you are talented and can do better than you have imagined, but what is the thing that is stopping you from doing your work? Is it the fear that you will make a joke out of yourself?

I know some of you are not afraid of failures but afraid of embarrassment. You fear that people will bully you if they knew your dreams and talent. You are fully confident about your talent but are afraid of people's reaction, am I right?

Some where your own people will stop you from achieving your dream life and you are not afraid of them stopping you but you are afraid of hurting them in the process of success.

The only thing from your past that you are holding is fear. You are afraid that maybe people from the past will become a problem in future or present. You are afraid that they will become an obstacle to your success.

If you detach yourself from the past and the people from the past, you can achieve your dream life more easily. You should detach yourself from all the things which don't serve you or are obstacles in your way.

• 58 •

Others judgement is not going to feed you or pay your bills, so it's better if you don't listen to anyone's judgement. What they think about you should not matter but what you think of yourself should matter.

You are going to judge yourself and feel low just because a guy who is not a man of his words, who always switches sides and is disloyal to every friend of his, said that you are not worthy enough?

The way you listen to others, why don't you listen to yourself like that? What is so wrong with listening to yourself? There are people out there who will make fun of you to look cool in front of others, who will judge you without any context.

People will show you respect only in front of your face there will be no genuine respect as you are not taking yourself seriously then why they will take you seriously?

The day you respect yourself others will also respect you. When you start treating yourself good others will also start treating you good. Remember it all starts within you; you are enough for yourself.

Don't judge yourself for doing something that you like because if you like it, do it. No one needs to know why you like it, and they don't even have the right to say that you should not do it. The people who gossip about you or judge you finds you interesting; that's why they are judging you instead of doing their own work.

Have you ever seen a millionaire judging someone for starting a business? No right! People who have nowhere to go and nothing to do are the ones who judge people for doing something they like.

In the end, the one who is going to be with you all the time is yourself only. Treat yourself the way you want to be treated by others.

WHY YOU?

You should never underestimate yourself because you may not see your worth, but others are aware of your worth. That's why sometimes a person who you think is better than you turns out to be your competitor. You may not think of him as a competitor, but he is looking at you as his competitor.

In today's world competition is everywhere even your closest person can be a competitor in disguise. They stay close to you to know your every move so that they can do better than you. Do not trust a person who always neglects your celebrations, he neglects your celebrations because he is burning from inside.

The only one you should trust should be you because you will never want failures for yourself, you will never be jealous of yourself. You know yourself better than anyone else so always listen to yourself and listen to your intuition.

I always believe that your body can sense danger, and it will constantly give you signals. Intuition is a way your body gives you a signal when it senses some danger or any negative energy. Nobody wants you to win as much as you want you to win.

You are always a target of someone who is not doing better than you; they target you because you are the kind of human they envy and always want to target you. The day they do better than you is the day they feel successful because their target was not doing better, but their target was to do better than you.

A wise advice I would like to give to you is to never do your work while keeping the result in your mind. The result is not your concern but not doing your work properly should be your concern. The day you stop working for result and start working for your betterment will be the day you will be successful.

Never try to better than anyone, try to be different. try to be better than yourself, try to be a better person than you were yesterday or the person you were a year ago. Trust me there is no better feeling than being your highest self.

The only thing you need to have is confidence, confidence to face everything coming at you bad or good. Confidence is the key to opportunities, success, basically you can have anything if you have enough confidence in yourself.

Be proud of yourself even if all you did was to survive. If no one is proud of you, be proud of yourself. Accepting yourself the way you are is a first step towards self-love. When you feel confident in your body, you are loving yourself.

It's not mandatory that your confidence should be real. You can fake it if you want to because the person in front of you doesn't know if your confidence is real or fake. It's kind of like "fake it till you make it," or in Gen-Z terms, we can say "delulu is the solulu," which translates into "delusion is the solution."

Confidence is good but over confidence is not good. There is a huge difference between confidence and arrogance, don't be too proud of yourself that your confidence turns into arrogance.

CHAPTER FIFTEEN

ITS JUST YOU!

Realizing that you are the only one who can be truly yours is such a blessing to your mindset. Create your life where you can you live peacefully, where nobody bothers you, where you can take your own decisions.

When you take responsibility of your own life, you have to work hard for providing yourself all the things which you have imagined for yourself. What changes are you willing to make to create the life of your dreams?

Are you willing to give up your laziness and the self-sabotaging habit of yours? Are you willing to give more time towards your goal and less time to stupidity? At least you can wake up early and exercise to keep your health good.

At least, can you leave all the toxic food that doesn't benefit you? Well, if you cannot do any of the above, then at least don't put energy into relationships and friendships if it's messing with your mental health.

Just imagine being financially stable and independent is also such a big win in life. Once you become financially independent, you cannot be controlled by anyone. I have seen in many cases that financial independence brings power and freedom to our lives.

When you are financially free, no one can throw a tantrum at you for being high maintenance. Winning at life also means staying away from people who create unnecessary drama in your life. Last but not least, a handsome and loyal man is also a win in life; it's completely optional. If you want, you can skip this part [just kidding]

Every day is a new life if you think of it as a new start. Accepting your past and choosing to move on and create a beautiful life in which you have peace of mind. The only person who you should live for should be you because sometimes even your best guardian can't help you because you are completely capable of helping yourself.

Don't let anyone ruin you, don't even allow yourself to ruin you. In our life 60% our parents ruin us, 20% friends and relatives ruin us and the rest we ruin it ourself. Don't worry about what four people will say about you instead worry about what you are feeding to your mind.

Imagine a day in your dream life, where there is no nuisance in the morning, waking up in your dream house, going to work which you absolutely love doing, coming back to home and hanging out with your friends or partner.

A productive day with lots of peace and happiness around you is all you can imagine for your dream life. To make your dream life come true, you have to work hard and maintain distance from all the things that keep you away from achieving your dream life.

Well, in the journey of your success, you have to make some promises to yourself that will help you.

Promises to me!

- Never cry for a person.
- Never endure disrespect from anyone.
- Always be happy; being healthy is a choice.
- Always help yourself first and then only help others.
- Once a person disrespects you, they no longer have any importance in your life.
- Don't make your day bad just because someone else's day is bad
- Always pamper yourself with lots of love.
- Never talk negative about yourself.

In the process of healing, you might feel lonely so here are some of the solo date ideas so that you can take yourself to date and can love yourself more.

Solo date ideas:
- Coffee date
- Beach date
- Movie date
- Bookstore date
- Journaling on beach
- Cooking for yourself
- Shopping
- A night walk
- Art gallery date
- Baking a cake
- Ice cream date
- Cycling
- Watching your favourite movie

I hope this will help you on your healing and self-love journey. I tried my best to make you love yourself; now it's your responsibility to love yourself enough.

Last but not the least, your self-respect should be important to you. Your ambition, your friends, your family who is truly yours should be important. Most important thing should be 'you' and your smile.

• 65 •

Last but not the least, your self-respect should be important to you. Your ambition, your friends, your family who is truly yours should be important. Most important thing should be 'you' and your smile.

A LETTER TO MYSELF

Dear myself,

I hope you are happy on this day and even if you are not, I hope after reading this letter you will be happy. I am so proud of you and your efforts and how you never give up. I am proud that you found your worth in the darkest moment. There is something about you that is so beautiful; that smile that you always carry.

Stop comparing yourself with your role models because one day you are going to be someone's role model. You have to achieve everything you have desired. You are completely capable of achieving all the things you have desired because there is a reason why it was planted in your heart, you are capable of achieving that dream that's why you dreamed about it.

There were times when I gave importance to others and not you. I am really sorry for all the injustice I did to you just to make others happy. I am really sorry for those days when I was fixing others when you, too, were bleeding. I am really sorry for those harsh words which I said to you instead of telling others. I am happy that now I have realised your worth, and now I will treat you so well that you will be happy again like your old self.

I wish I could go back in time and take a stand for you so that you don't have to do the things in which you were not comfortable. I wish I could go back in time and love you a little more in that moment when you were helpless instead of complaining. I am really sorry that I couldn't protect you back then.

Don't be like me anymore, please. Be the person you always wanted to be and live your life the best way you can. Don't depend on people's validation; you are not bound by anyone or anything. Break the toxic boundaries and fly, my dear.

If you ever feel like giving up just read this letter it will remind you of those days when you were at your lowest but you still didn't give up. For you I will fight every obstacle. I hope you are living the life which I imagined, I hope you are getting everything which I desired. I hope you have people around you who loves you for who you are.

I really don't know how you would look in future but I hope you are more beautiful inside and outside. I hope everything is going according to your wish and I wish you live a very amazing life in future and present.

Whatever your dream is, do it; don't waste your time thinking of the consequences. Just do it. Don't be afraid to dream big because we cannot achieve anything without dreaming about it. If you can dream it, then you can also achieve it; just believe in yourself.

Lastly, love yourself more and don't be insecure about any of your traits. You are completely gorgeous; you just can't see it, just like a butterfly who cannot see her own beautiful wings, but the whole world is aware of how beautiful the butterfly is.

Always remember, even if no one is proud of you, I will always be proud of you; you are my inspiration.

Love you so much!

-From your younger self to the new one

Credits

Pictures from chapters:-

Chapter 1
https://pin.it/5sFoiCt18

Chapter 2
https://pin.it/5hPPc7KG6

Chapter 3
https://pin.it/qil4Tcvae

Chapter 4
https://pin.it/7rbPtggD9

Chapter 5
https://pin.it/7rbPtggD9

The images used in the book used to enhance the beauty of the book are not of author but are taken from Pinterest.

www.ingramcontent.com/pod-product-compliance
Lightning Source LLC
Chambersburg PA
CBHW040742120726
48007CB00007B/73